CW01651300

Tom of Finland

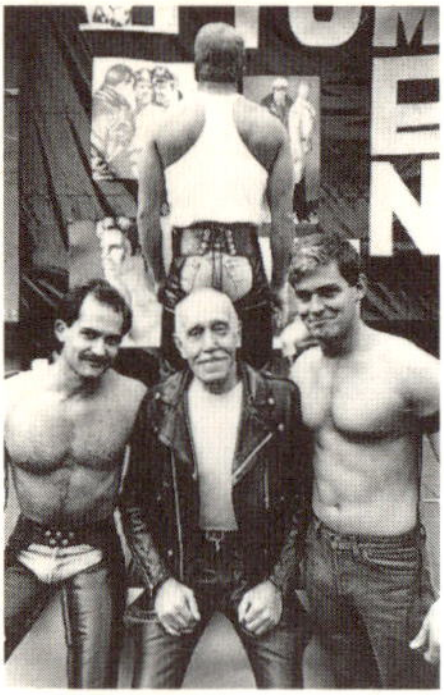
Tom at the Eagle Bar, San Francisco 1982
Photo: Robert Purzan

Tom of Finland was born on the south coast of Finland in 1920. His name was originally Touko, Finnish for May, the month in which he was born. At the age of five he was already drawing cartoon figures, and in his youth developed a particular interest in literature and music.

In 1939, he moved to Helsinki to study at art college, after which he did free-lance artwork in advertising, supplementing his income by playing piano in bars and at parties. Meanwhile, he was doing his own drawings.

In late 1956 Touko sent a selection of these drawings to a well-known American gay magazine. Afraid of the possible consequences, he signed his drawings »Tom of Finland« – the name by which he subsequently became famous. The editor was enthusiastic, and a year later a laughing lumberjack drawn by Tom graced the cover of »Physique Pictorial«. The picture was a sensation, and Tom's work – which he himself had always referred to as »dirty drawings« – rapidly became popular. When Tom's work was first published, homosexuals thought they had to be imitation women. Thirty-five years later, gays were much more likely to be masculinity personified. Tom of Finland died of a stroke on 7 November 1991. His art played its part in promoting the self-confidence and positive upheat openness that has evolved in the gay community over the past 20 years. »I work very hard, so as to be sure that the men I draw at their love-games are proud men having happy sex.«

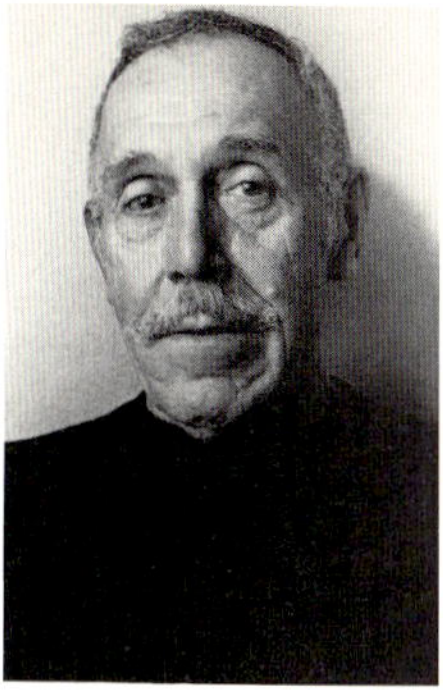

Tom of Finland, 1978
Photo: Robert Mapplethorpe
© Robert Mapplethorpe Foundation, 1978

Tom of Finland wurde 1920 an der Südküste Finnlands geboren. Sein ursprünglicher Vorname ist Touko, was im Finnischen soviel wie Mai heißt. Bereits im Alter von fünf Jahren zeichnete er Comics. Darüber hinaus galt sein besonderes Interesse der Literatur und Musik. Im Jahre 1939 zog es ihn nach Helsinki , wo er sich an der Kunsthochschule einschrieb. Nach Beendigung dieser Ausbildung arbeitete Touko freischaffend in der Werbung. Zusätzlich verdiente er seinen Lebensunterhalt als Pianist in Bars und auf Parties. Unabhängig davon entstehen Zeichnungen. Ende 1956 schickte Touko auf Drängen eines Freundes eine Auswahl seiner Blätter an ein bekanntes amerikanisches Schwulenmagazin. Aus Angst vor Repressalien signierte er diese mit »Tom of Finland«, dem Namen, unter dem er schließlich berühmt werden sollte. Der Herausgeber war begeistert, so daß ein Jahr später ein lachender Holzfäller von Tom das Cover von »Physique Pictorial« schmückte. Das Bild war eine Sensation, und seine Arbeiten, die Tom immer wieder als »schmutzige Zeichnungen« bezeichnet hat, wurden schnell populär. Tom of Finland starb am 7. November 1991 an einem Schlaganfall. Seine Kunst hat ihren Teil dazu beigetragen, daß die Homosexuellenszene in den letzten 20 Jahren zu einem neuen Selbstbewußtsein gefunden hat. »Ich arbeite sehr hart, um sicherzugehen, daß die Männer, die ich beim Liebesspiel zeichne, stolze Männer sind, die glücklichen Sex haben.«

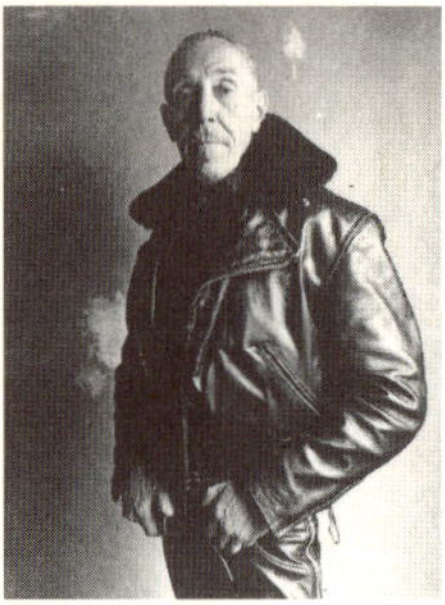

Tom of Finland, Los Angeles, c. 1980
Photo: anonymous

Tom of Finland est né en 1920 sur la côte sud de la Finlande. En fait, il se nomme Touko, ce qui signifie «mai» en finnois. A cinq ans, il dessine déjà des bandes dessinées et s'intéresse tout particulièrement à la littérature et à la musique. En 1939, il part pour Helsinki et s'inscrit à la faculté des Beaux-Arts. Après avoir terminé ses études il va travailler de manière indépendante dans la publicité.

Il gagne également sa vie en jouant du piano dans les bars et dans les soirées. Il dessine pendant ses loisirs. Fin 1956, il envoie quelques dessins à un magazine américain spécialisé. Mais, l'époque incitant à la prudence, il les signe «Tom of Finland», un nom qui va devenir célèbre.

Les dessins plaisent tellement à l'éditeur qu'un an plus tard, c'est un dessin de Tom, un bûcheron riant aux éclats, qui va orner la couverture du «Physique Pictorial». Il a beaucoup de succès, et les travaux de Tom, ses «dessins sales» selon ses propres termes, vont acquérir une grande popularité. A l'époque où Tom commença à publier ses dessins, les homosexuels pensaient qu'ils devaient imiter les femmes; ils étaient des êtres de l'ombre. Tom of Finland, gravement malade, meurt d'une attaque d'apoplexie le 7 novembre 1991. Son œuvre a contribué à ce que les homosexuels se trouvent une nouvelle identité au cours des vingt dernières années. «Je travaille très dur pour affirmer que les hommes que j'ai dessinés en train de faire l'amour sont des hommes fiers et le font dans la joie!»

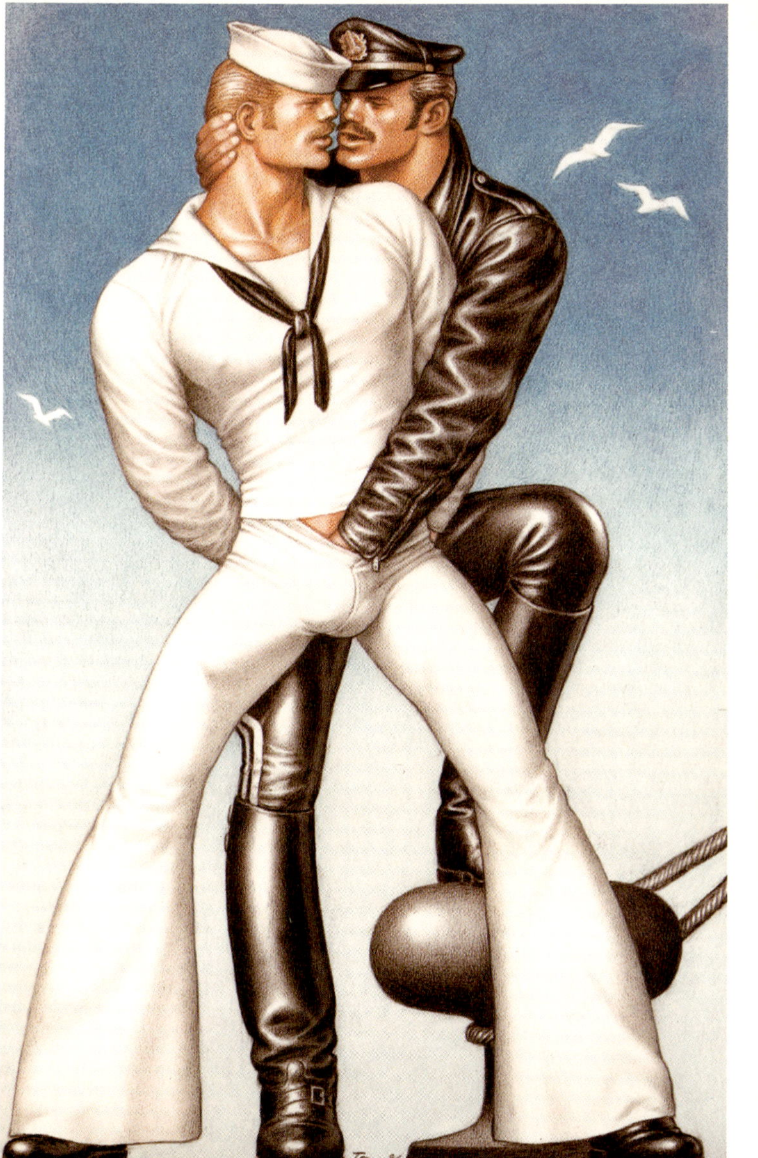
Tom - 86

Tom of Finland: Drawing, 1986

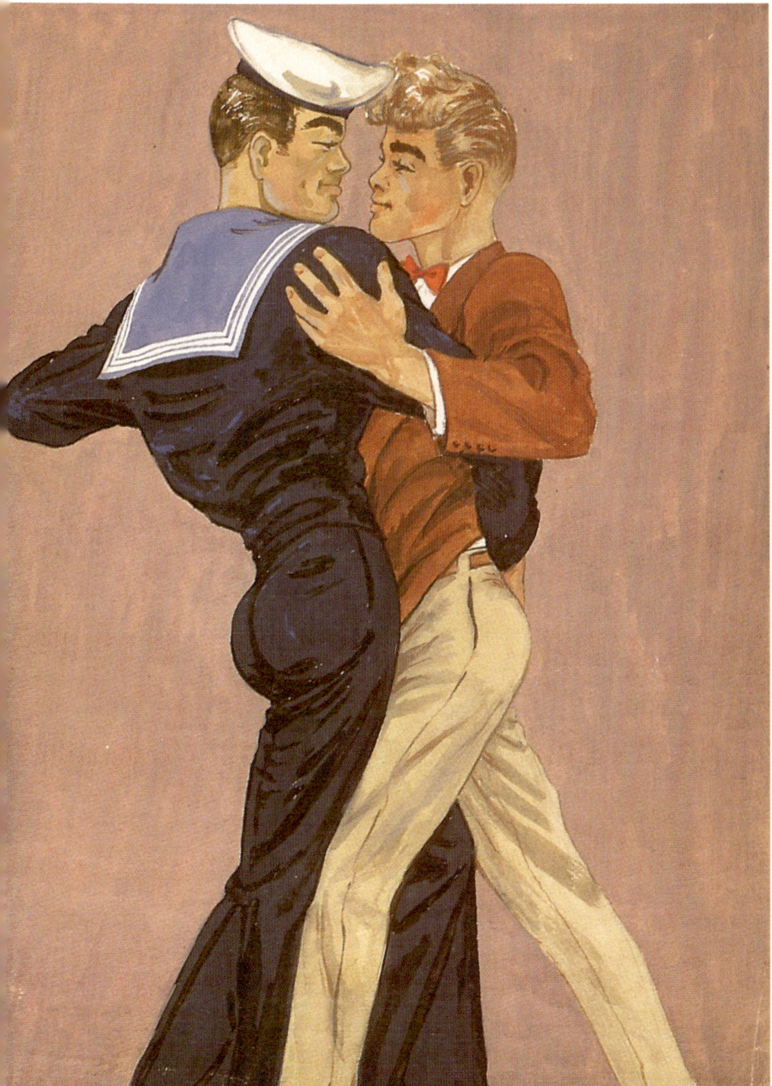

Tom of Finland: Drawing, 1947

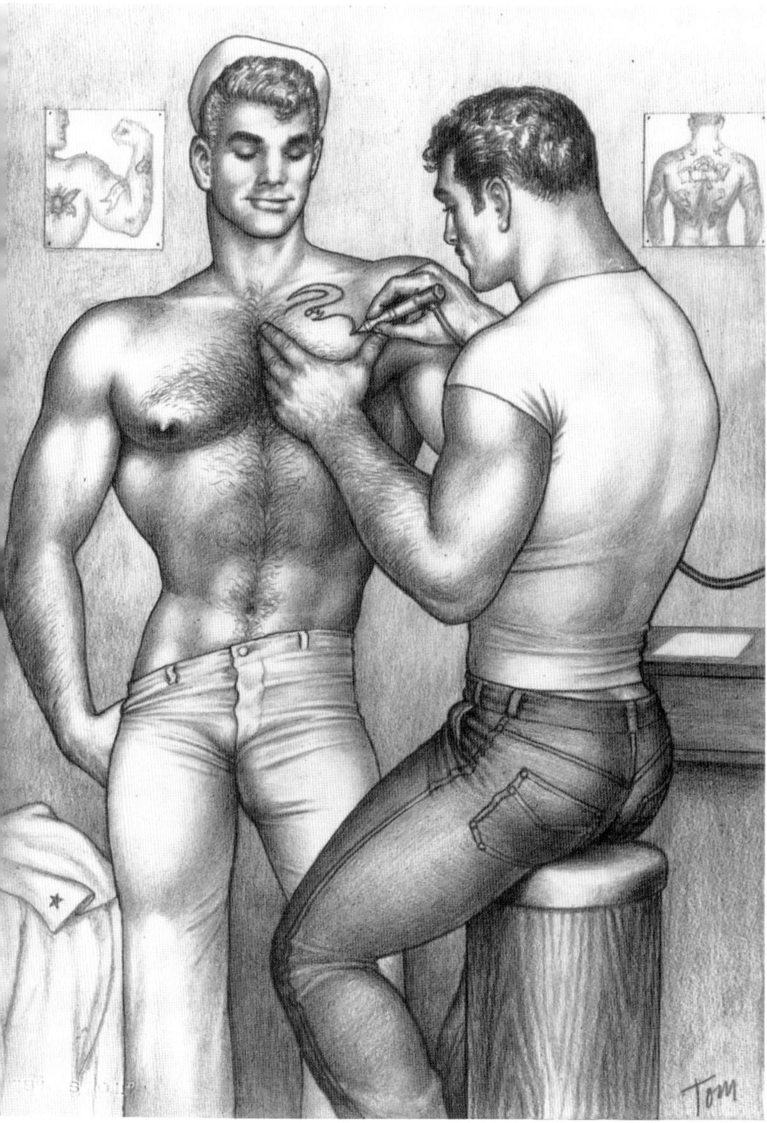
Tom

Tom of Finland: Drawing, 1962

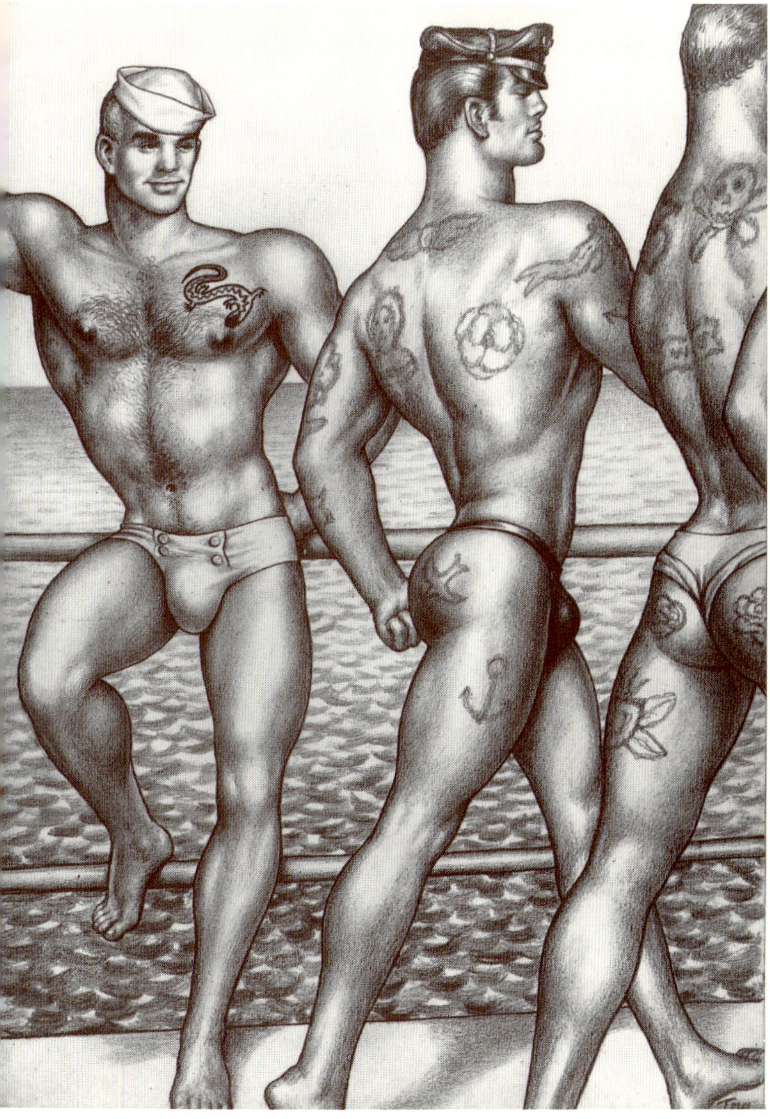

Tom of Finland: Drawing, 1962

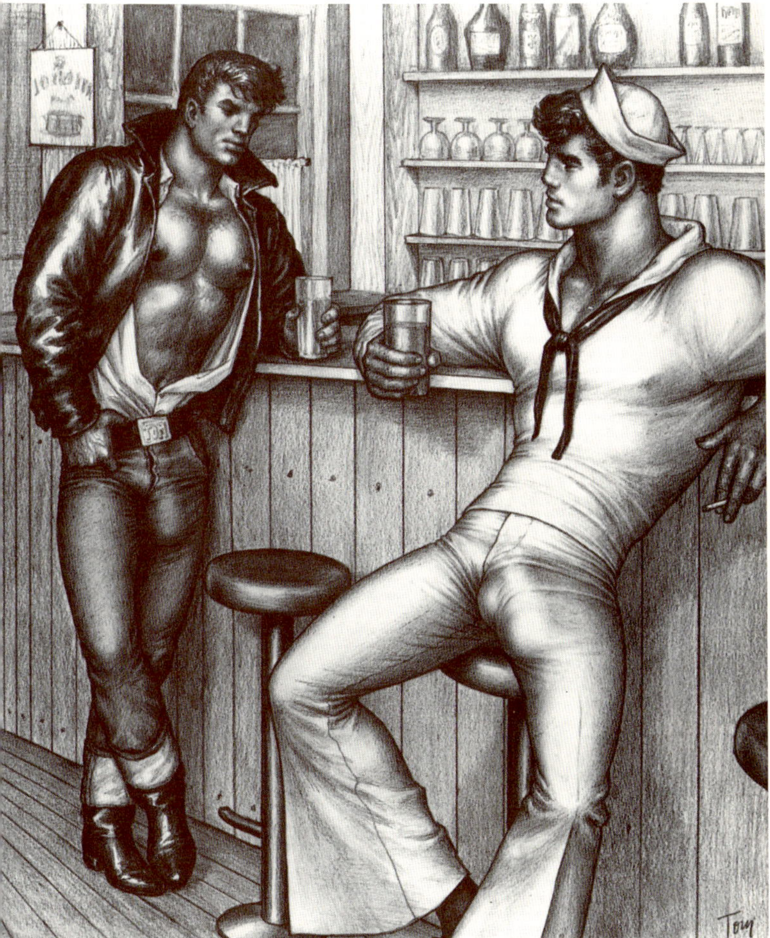
Tom

Tom of Finland: Drawing, 1962

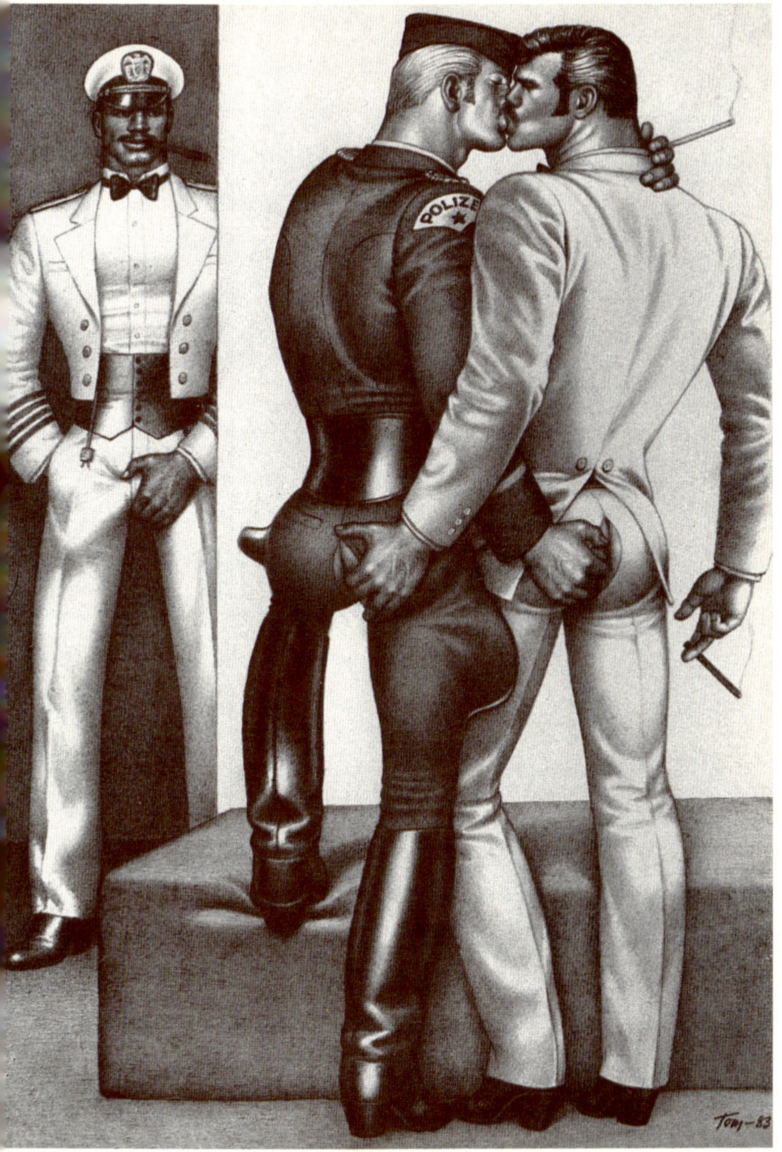
POLIZE
Tom-83

Tom of Finland: Drawing, 1983

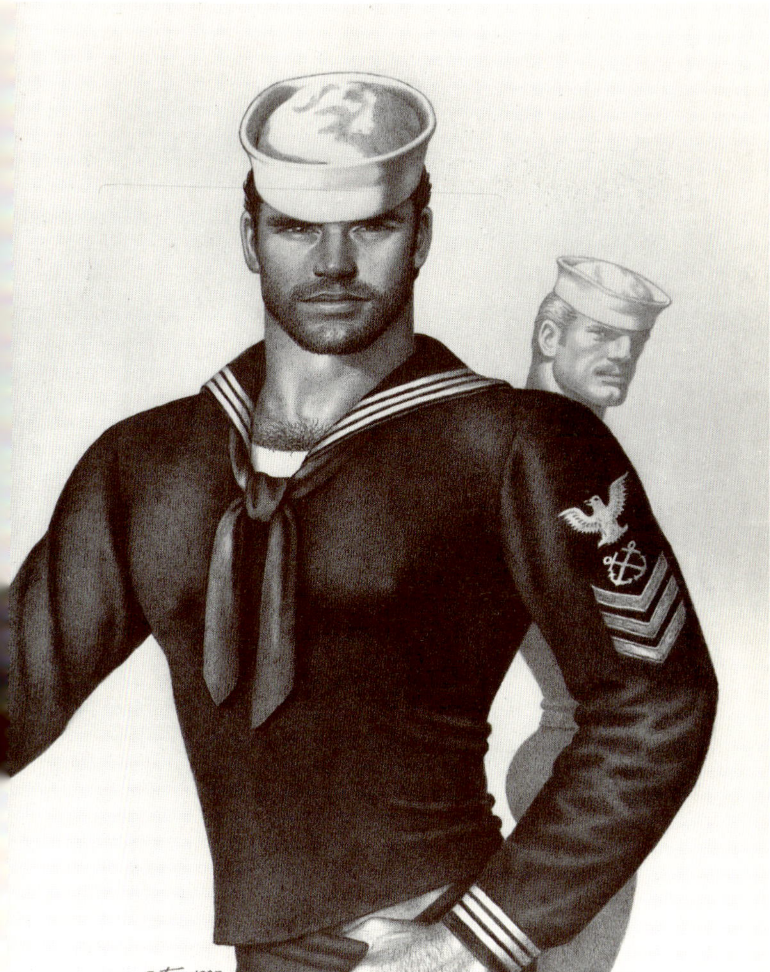
©Tom 1985

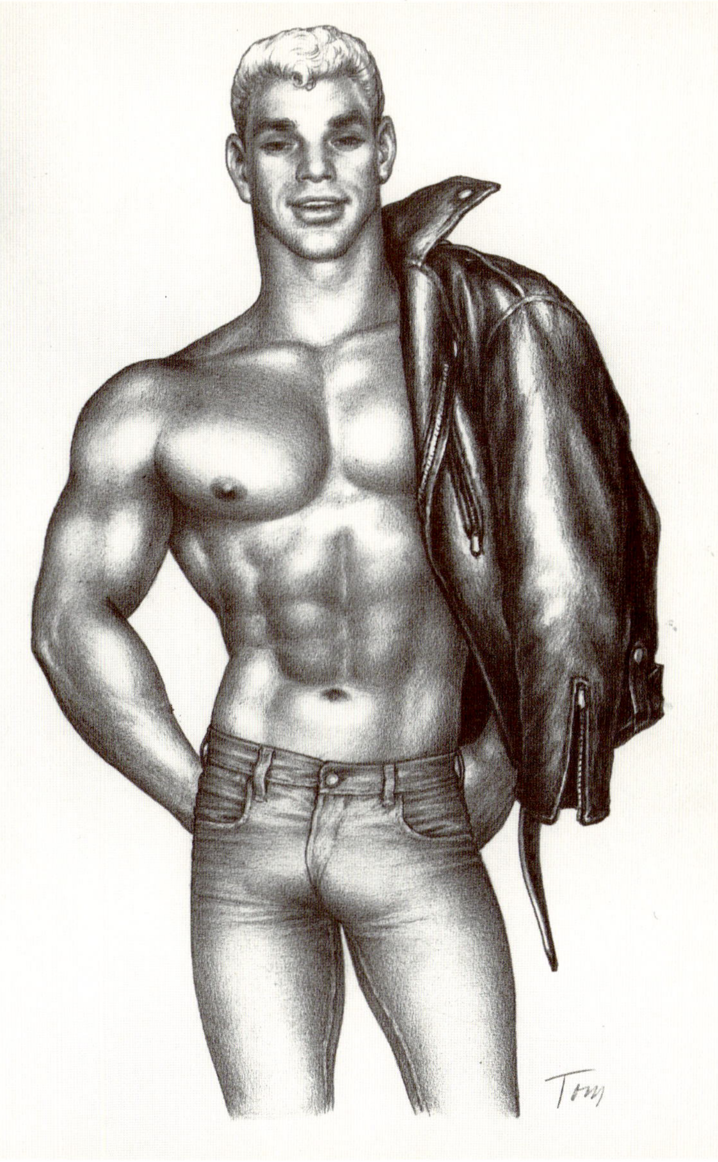
Tom

Tom of Finland: Drawing, 1961

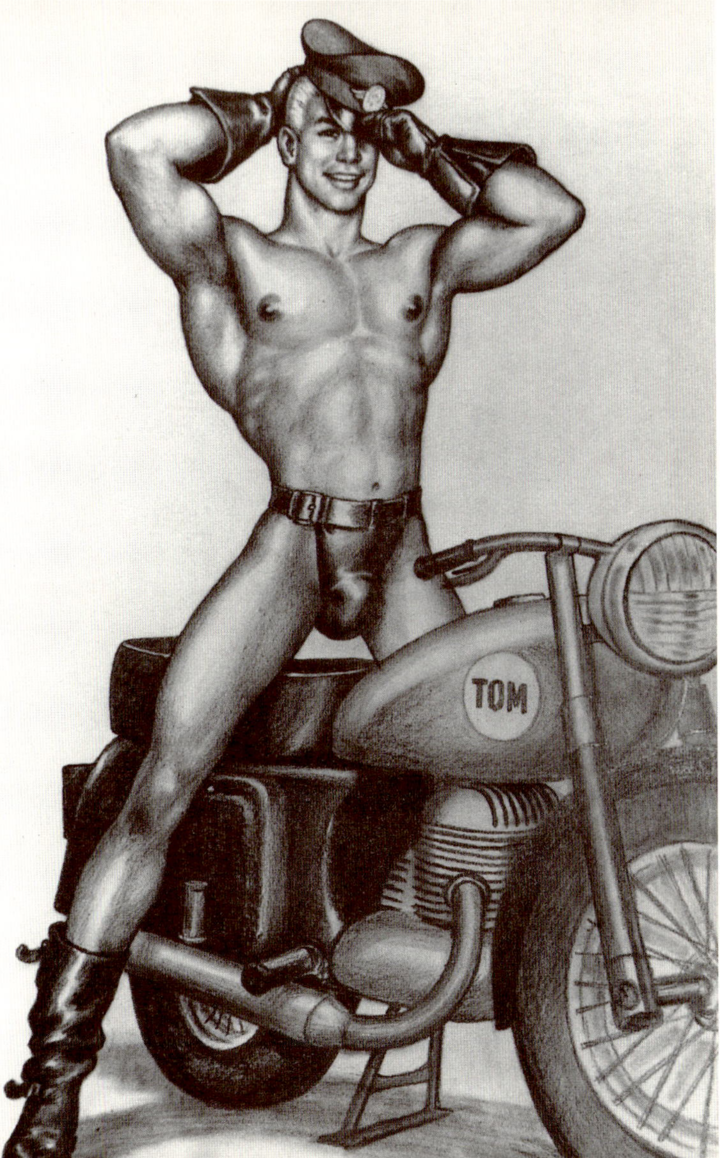
TOM

Tom of Finland: Drawing, 1960

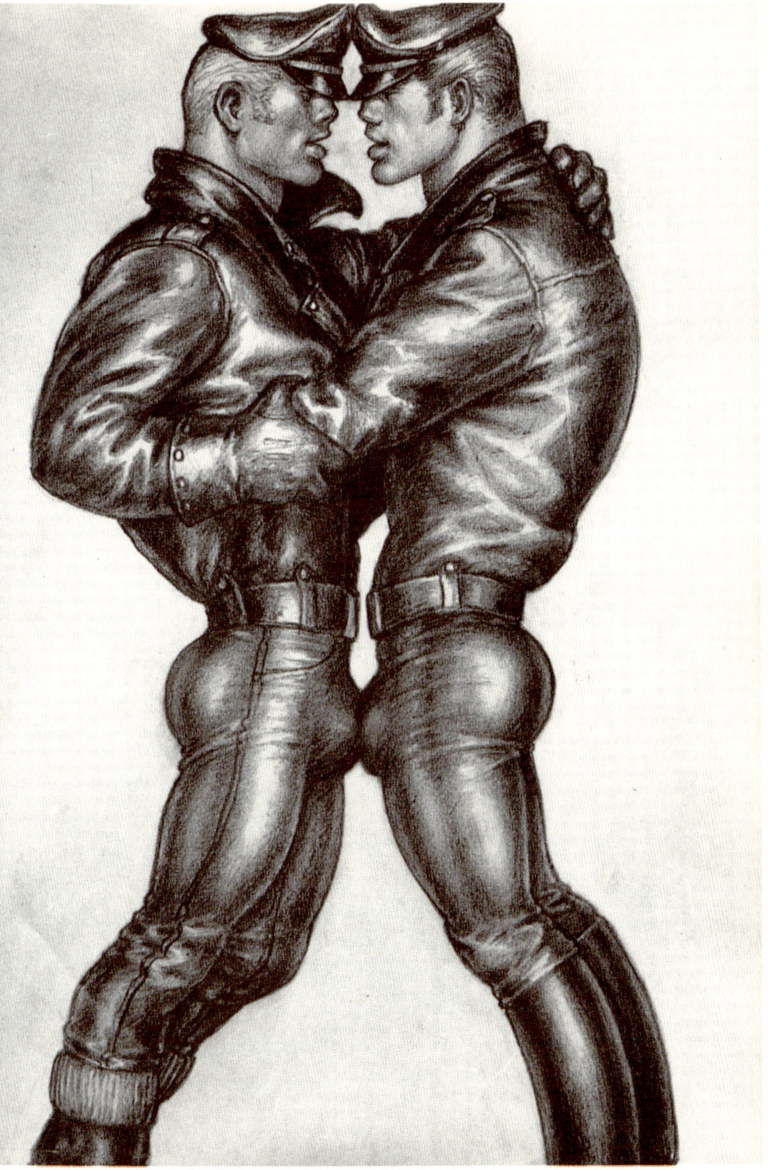

Tom of Finland: Drawing, 1963

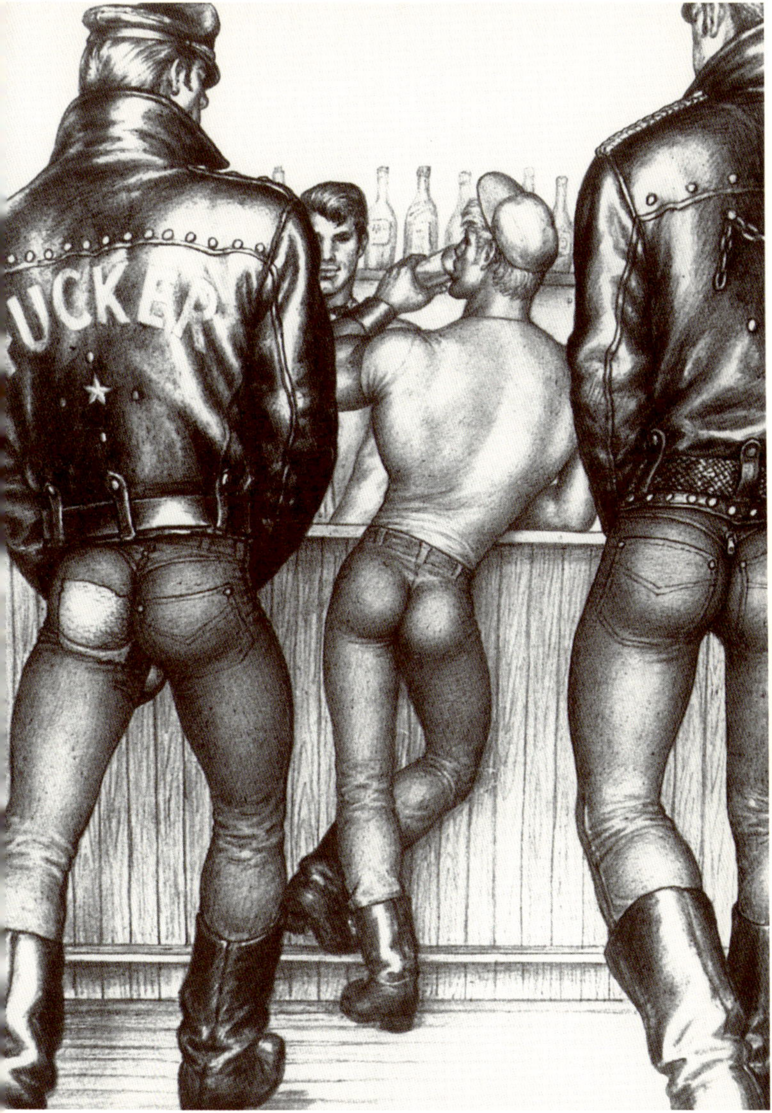
UCKER

© Benedikt Taschen

Tom of Finland: Drawing, 1965
© The Tom of Finland Foundation Inc., Los Angeles

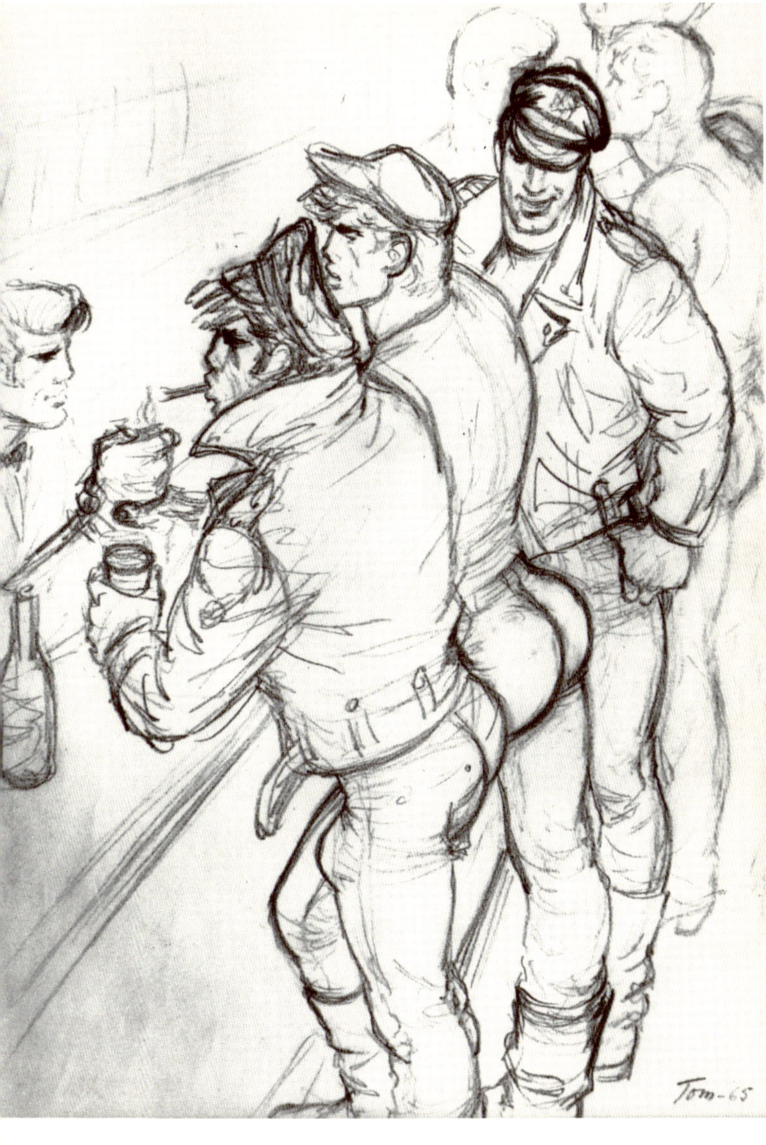
Tom-65

Tom of Finland: Drawing, 1965

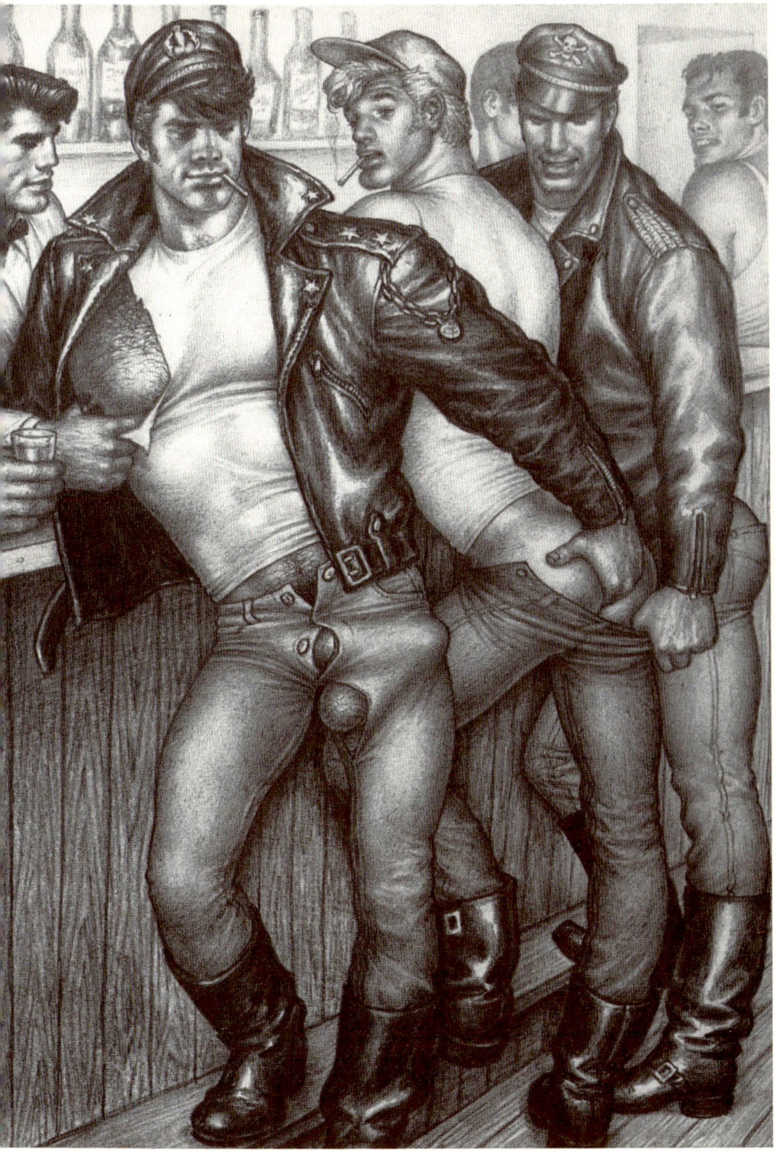

Tom of Finland: Drawing, 1965

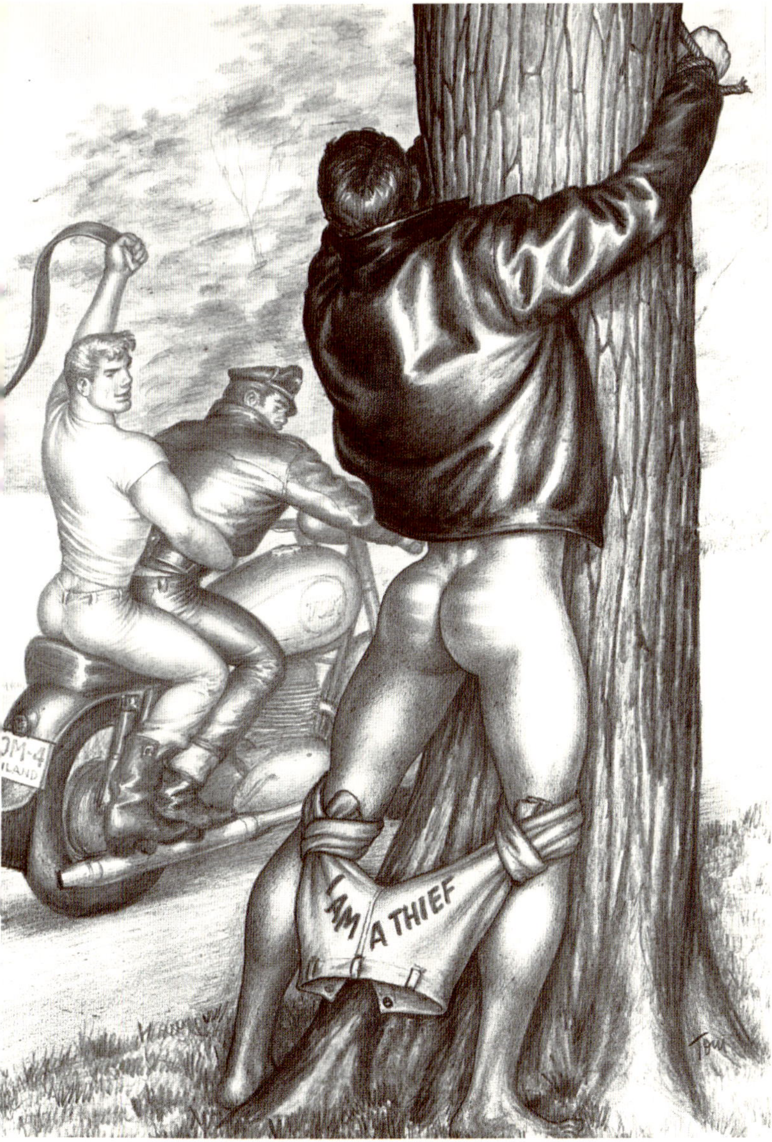
I AM A THIEF
Tom

Tom of Finland: Drawing, 1964

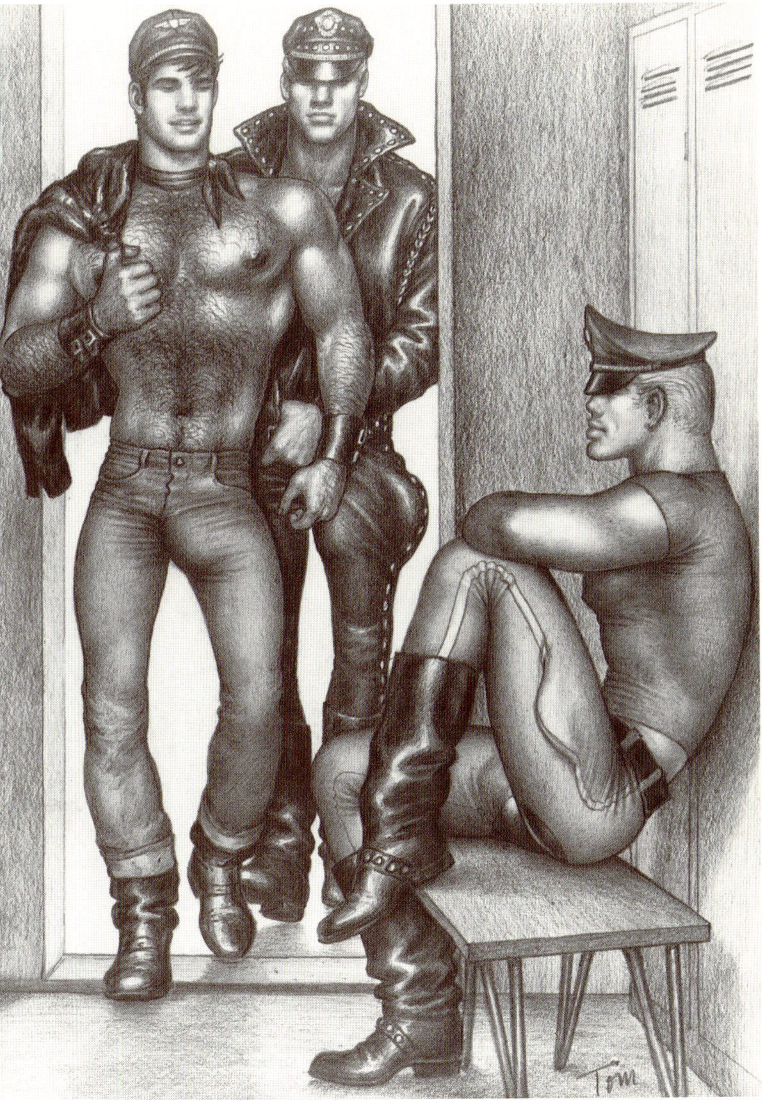
Tom

Tom of Finland: Drawing, 1965

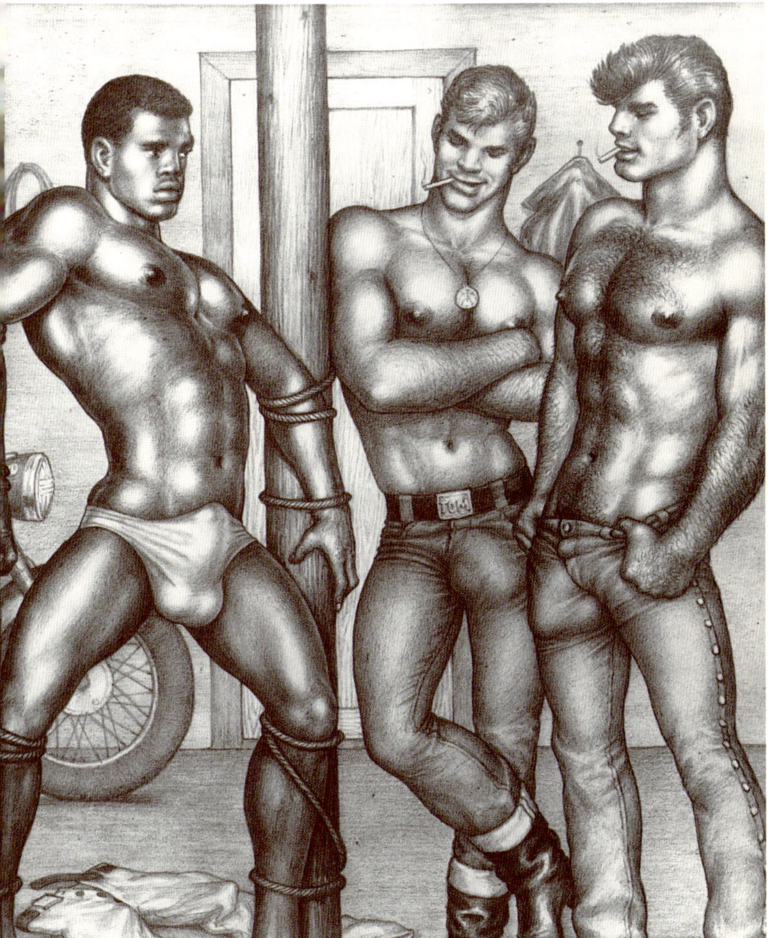
TOM
Tom

Tom of Finland: Drawing, 1962

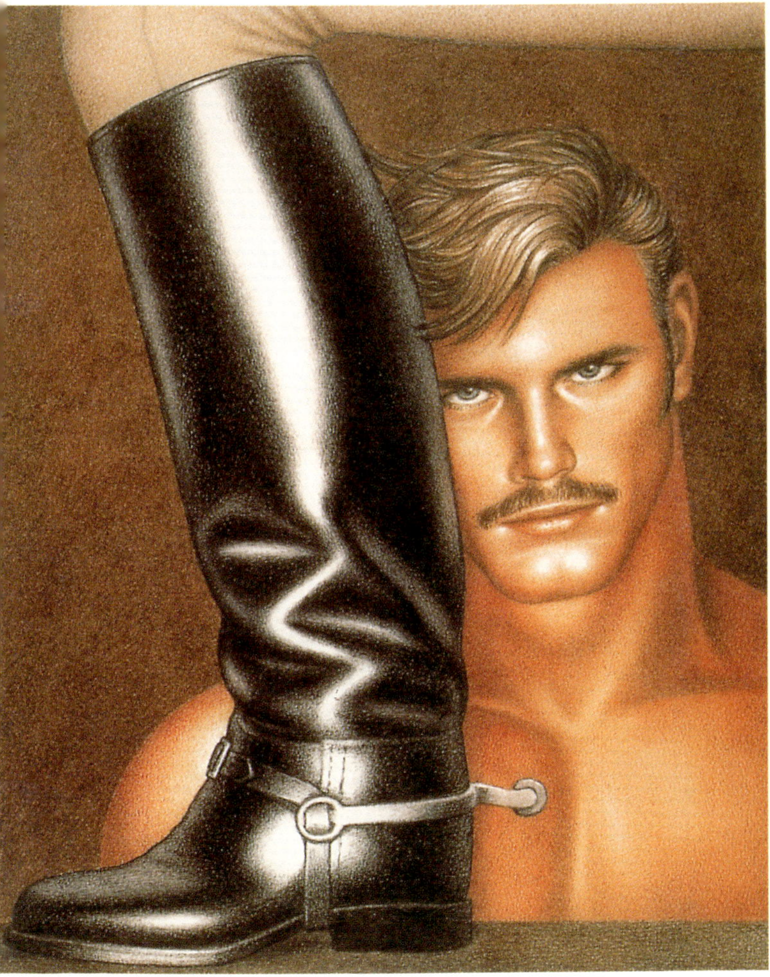

Tom of Finland: Drawing, 1982

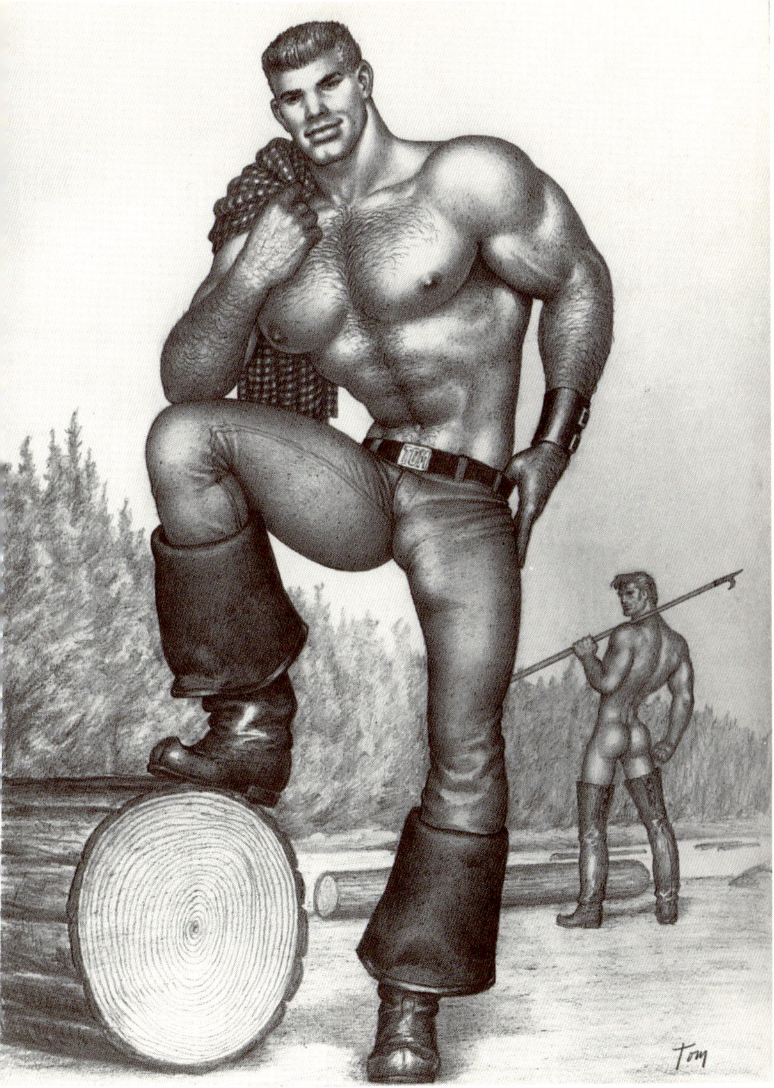
Tom

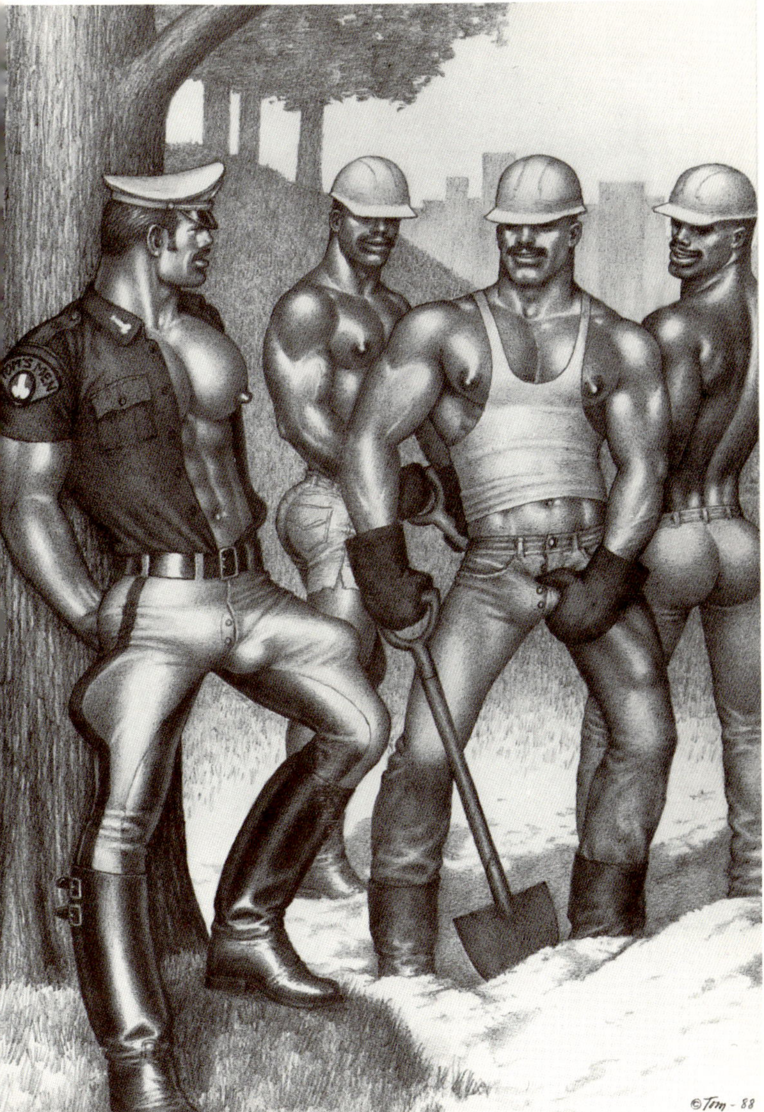
©Tom - 88

Tom of Finland: Drawing, 1988

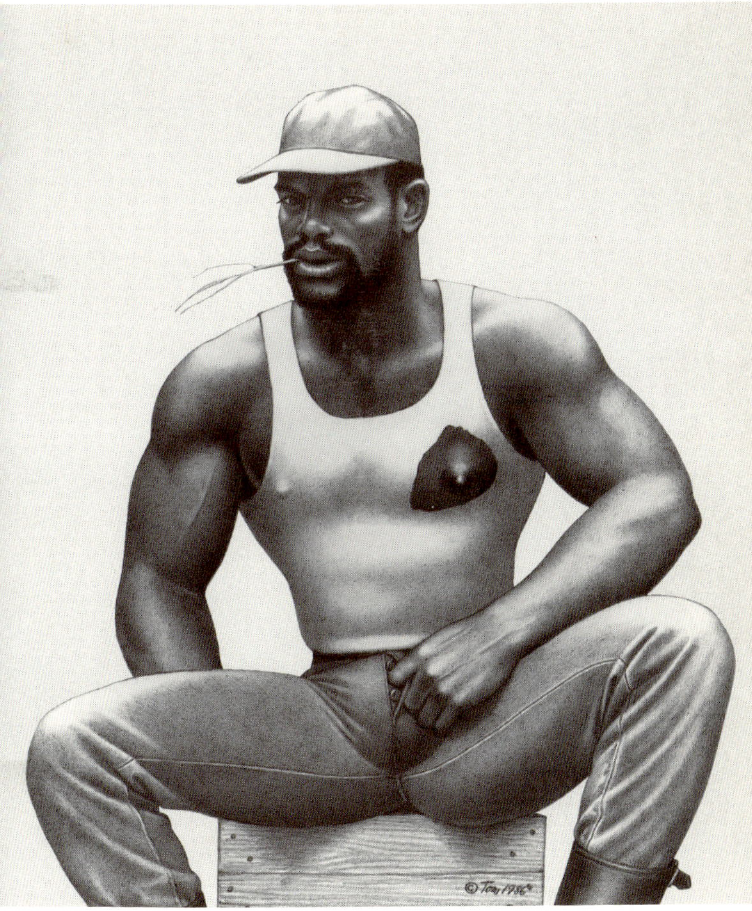
©Tom 1986

Tom of Finland: Drawing, 1986

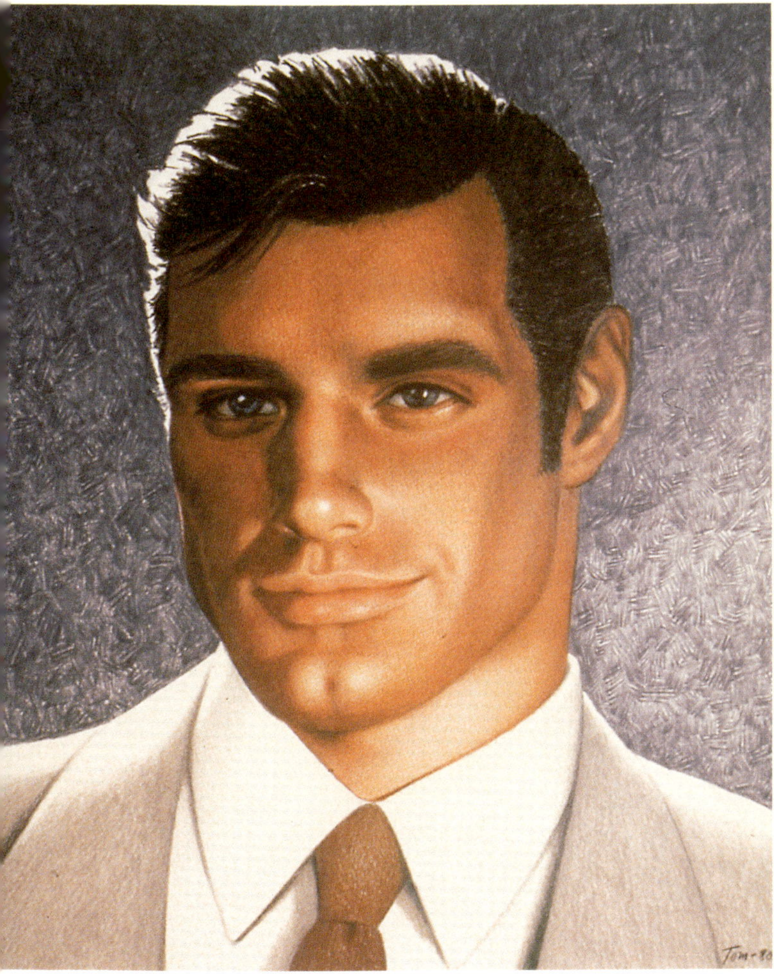

Tom of Finland: Drawing, 1980

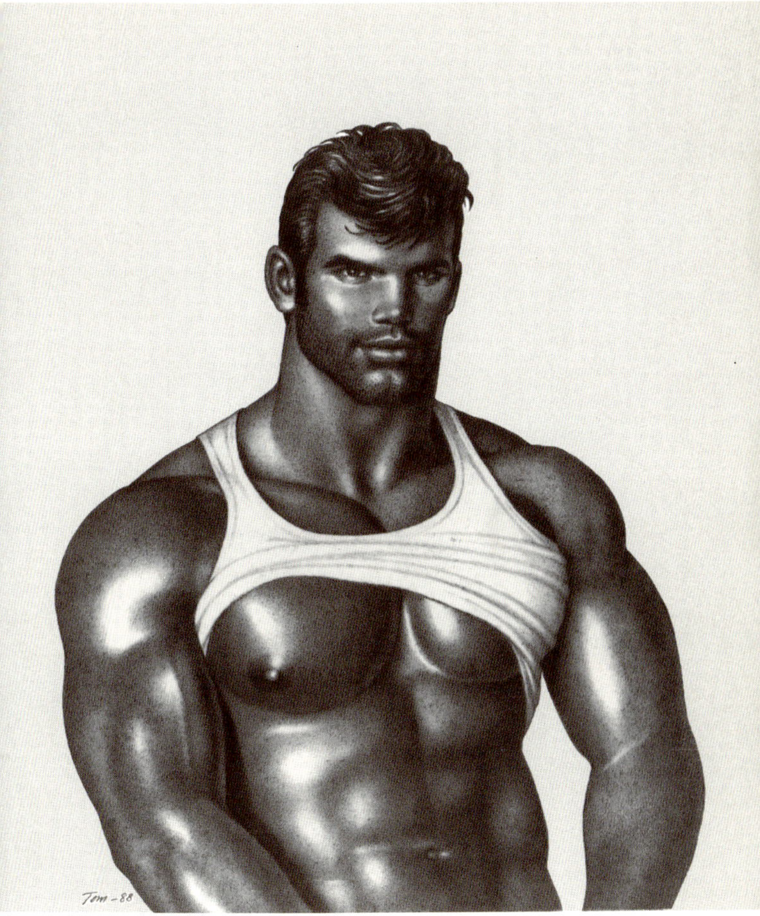
Tom -88

Tom of Finland: Drawing, 1988

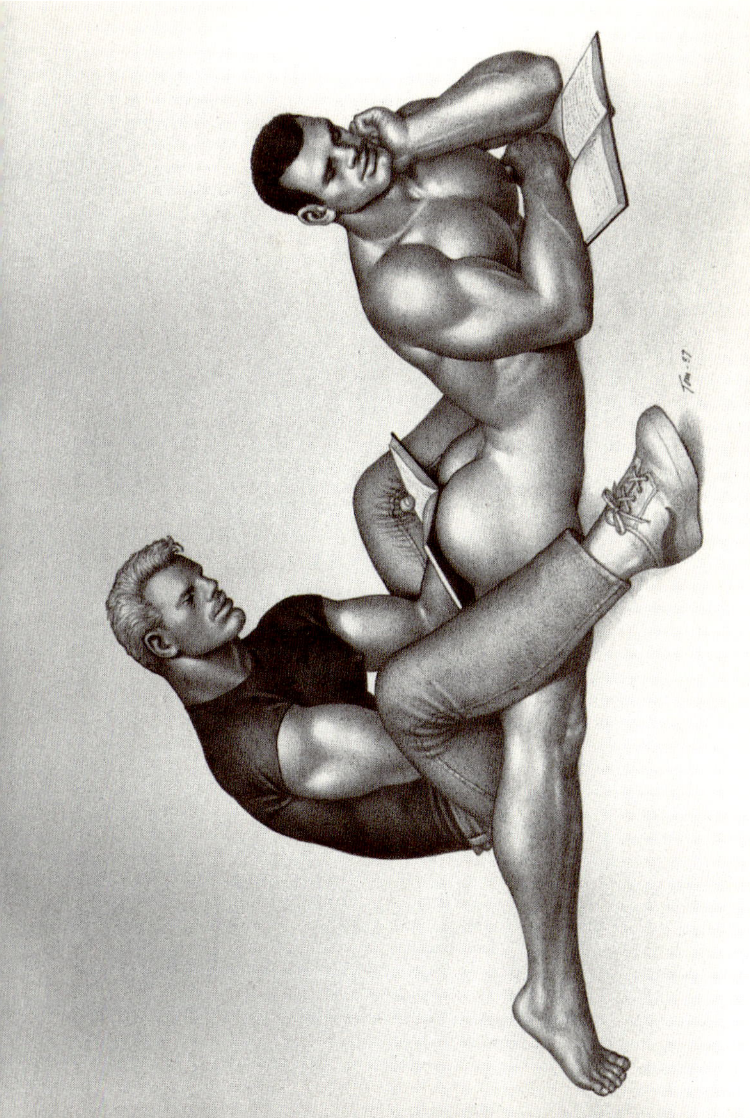

Tom of Finland: Drawing, 1987

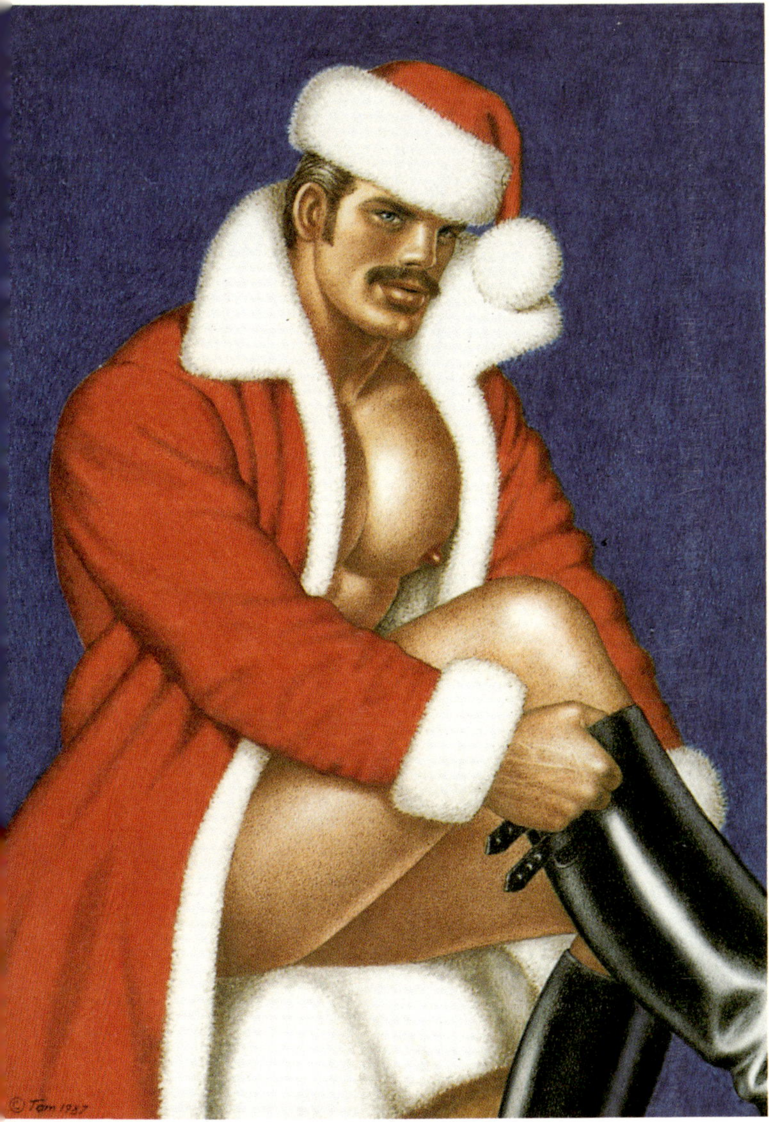
© Tom

Tom of Finland: Drawing, 1987

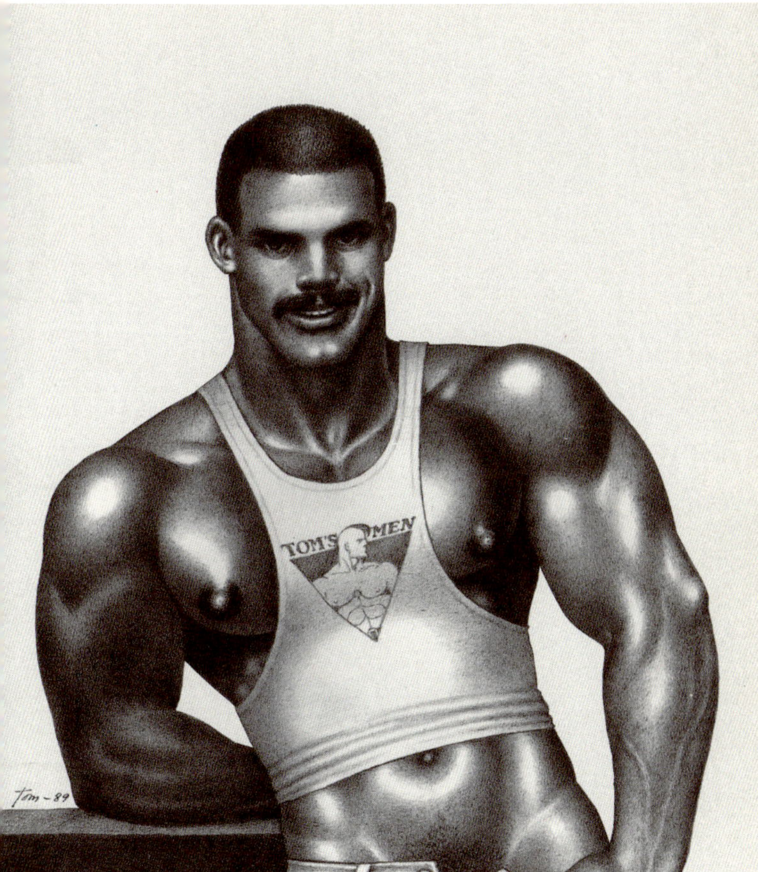
TOM'S MEN
Tom - 89

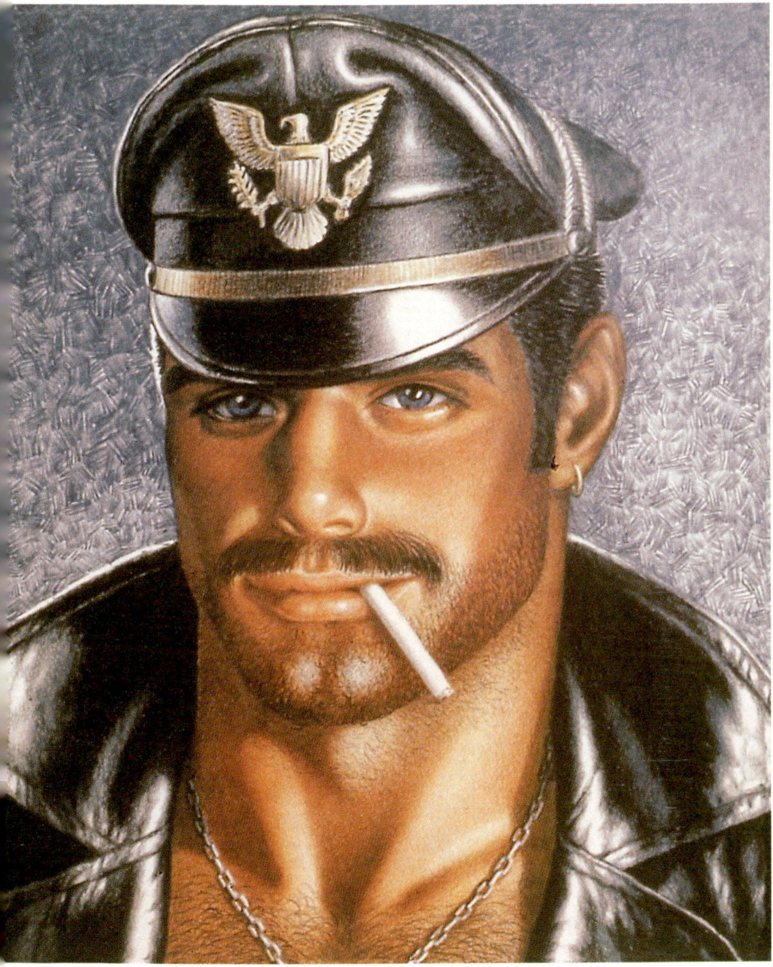

Tom of Finland: Drawing, 1981

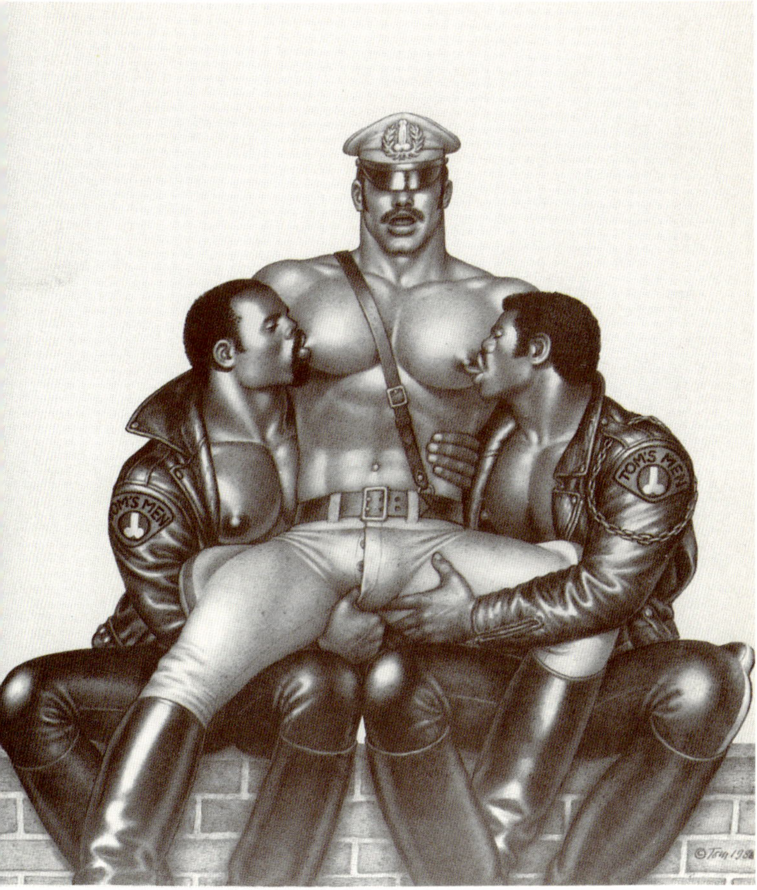
TOM'S MEN
TOM'S MEN

Tom of Finland: Drawing, 1986

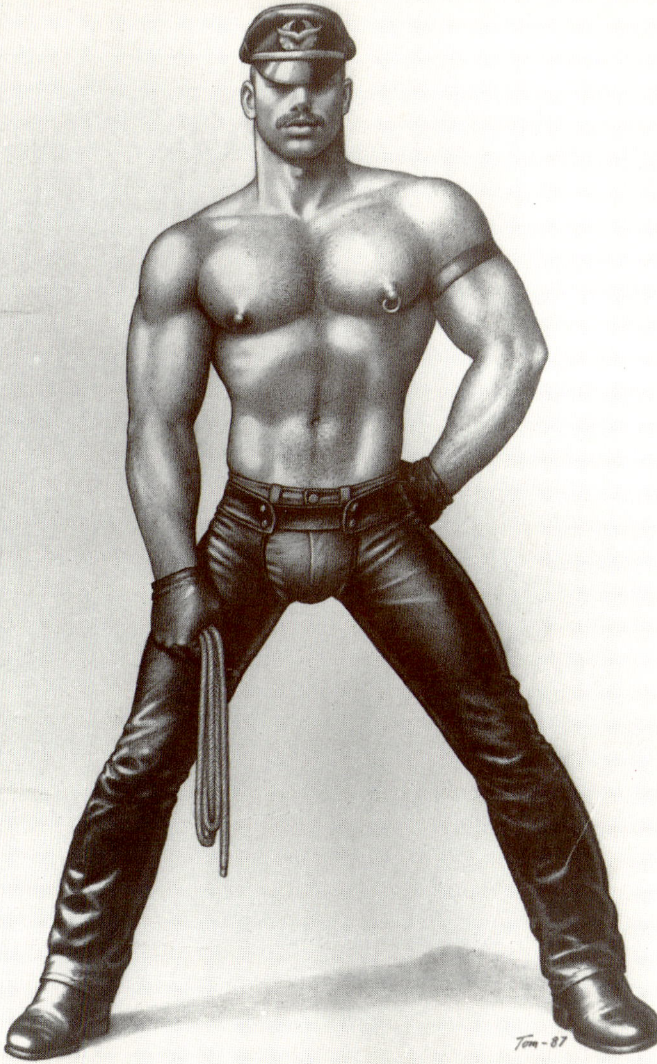
Tom-87

Tom of Finland: Drawing, 1987

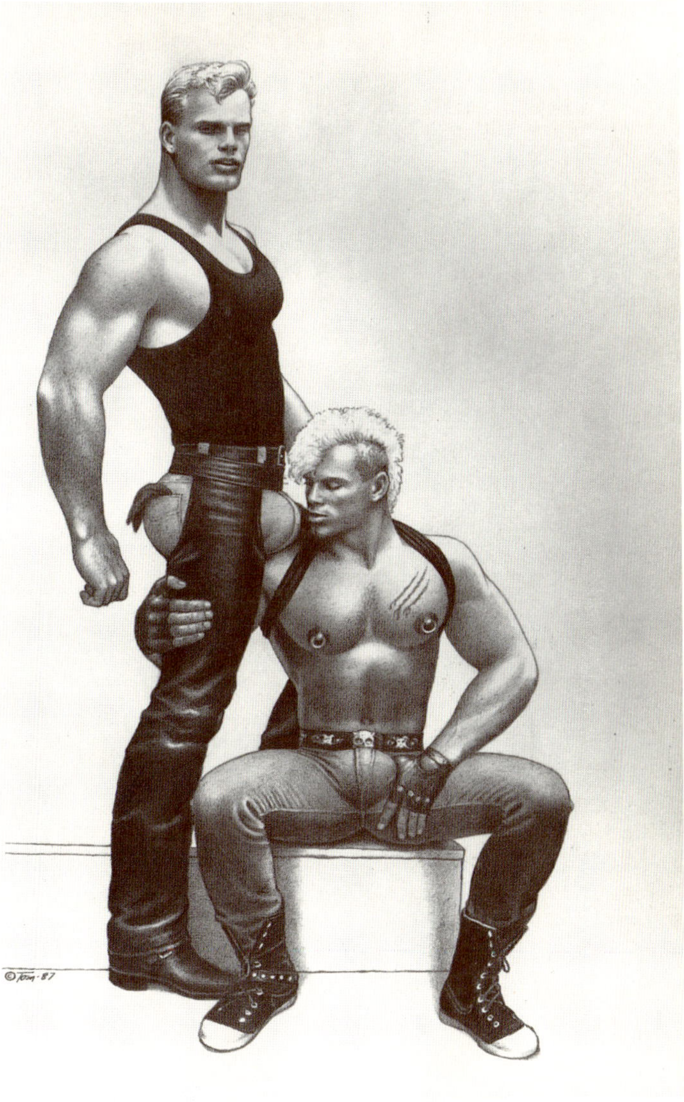
©Tom·87

Tom of Finland: Drawing, 1987

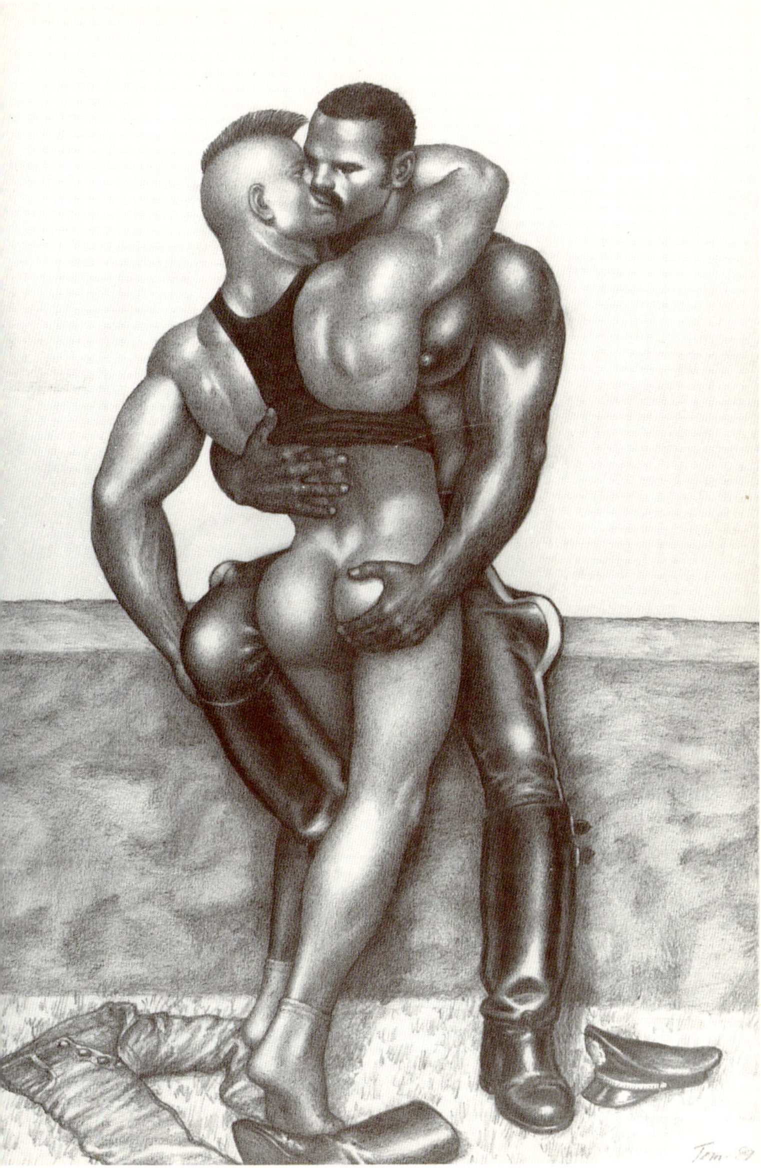

Tom of Finland: Drawing, 1989